Facts About the Platypus

By Lisa Strattin

© 2019 Lisa Strattin

FREE BOOK

FOR ALL SUBSCRIBERS

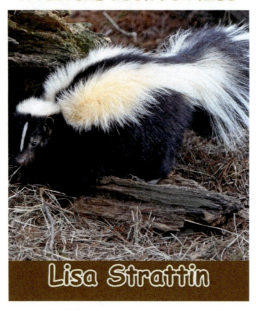

LisaStrattin.com/Subscribe-Here

Facts for Kids Picture Books by Lisa Strattin

Little Blue Penguin, Vol 92

Chipmunk, Vol 5

Frilled Lizard, Vol 39

Blue and Gold Macaw, Vol 13

Poison Dart Frogs, Vol 50

Blue Tarantula, Vol 115

African Elephants, Vol 8

Amur Leopard, Vol 89

Sabre Tooth Tiger, Vol 167

Baboon, Vol 174

Sign Up for New Release Emails Here

http://LisaStrattin.com/subscribe-here

COVER IMAGE

ADDITIONAL IMAGES

Contents

INTRODUCTION

The Platypus, also called the Duck-Billed Platypus, is a small semi-aquatic mammal native to the eastern coast of Australia. Known for their unique appearance, the Platypus belongs to a small group of mammals called monotremes.

The Platypus is one of only a few mammals known to lay eggs instead of giving birth to live young. For this reason, they were not considered mammals for a long time after they were discovered. When the first Platypus arrived in Britain in 1798, people thought it was not real at all since it looks like it is a part mammal and part bird.

CHARACTERISTICS

They are nocturnal hunters that are able to close their eyes, ears and nostrils when diving down to the river bed to find food. During the day, they rest in burrows dug into the river banks. There are two different burrows used by them; one for resting and one for incubating eggs and feeding their babies.

APPEARANCE

The Platypus has a small, streamlined body covered in short, dense waterproof fur that can be dark brown on their back with a light brown or silver underside and a plum-colored middle. They have short limbs with partially webbed hind feet and a broad, flat tail, like the tail of a beaver, that are used just like boat rudders when they are underwater. Their front feet are fully webbed and help them shoot through the water.

Their large, broad bill looks like the beak of a duck! It is soft and pliable, with lots of sensory receptors that help them to sense and locate their food.

REPRODUCTION

Breeding takes place between late winter and early spring, July through October, in the water, with males using their poison spurs to deliver a painful dose of poison to rival males. As part of their courtship, females carry bundles of wet leaves to their incubation chamber at the end of their burrow and then plug the tunnel closed with dirt.

A female lays one to three small, eggs that are less than 1 inch in size, soft and leathery. After incubating the eggs for around 10 days, the young hatch measuring less than 1/2 inch long, blind, hairless and with only blunt buds for legs. They are nursed by their mother for up to 5 months, then they begin eating solid food.

Males have a poison spur on each hind foot that they use to drive away rival males.

LIFE SPAN

Platypuses tend to live for around 10 years in the wild but can reach ages of 17 or more when in captivity.

SIZE

An adult platypus weighs between 1.5 to 5.5 pounds and males are usually larger than the females.

HABITAT

They are found on the east coast of Australia from Cooktown in Queensland in the north, all the way down to the island of Tasmania in the south and have also been introduced to Kangaroo Island in southern Australia.

They live in streams and rivers, and some lakes as long as there are banks for digging their burrows and a permanent water source. Their home ranges will depend on the specific river system and can vary in size from less than half a mile to more than 4 miles. One's range can overlap ranges of others despite their solitary nature.

DIET

They are carnivorous and their diet is almost completely the available bottom-dwelling aquatic creatures where the platypus lives. Young insects are the majority of their diet, as well as some small freshwater crustaceans, snails, tadpoles and small fish.

Because their eyes, ears and nostrils are closed when they are underwater, the Platypus relies solely on its sensitive bill to find food. When hunting food, they store food in cheek pouches, then grind the food using horny ridges that they have instead of teeth.

ENEMIES

They protect themselves from predators when resting during the day in their riverbank burrows. However, because they are small, they are preyed upon by a number of different animals in their home ranges. Their most common predators include: birds of prey like the hawks and eagles, large mammals including dingoes, dogs, cats and Tasmanian Devils, as well as reptiles like snakes, monitor lizards and crocodiles.

Despite the fact that they are widespread and considered very common in some areas, they were hunted to almost extinction in the 18th century.

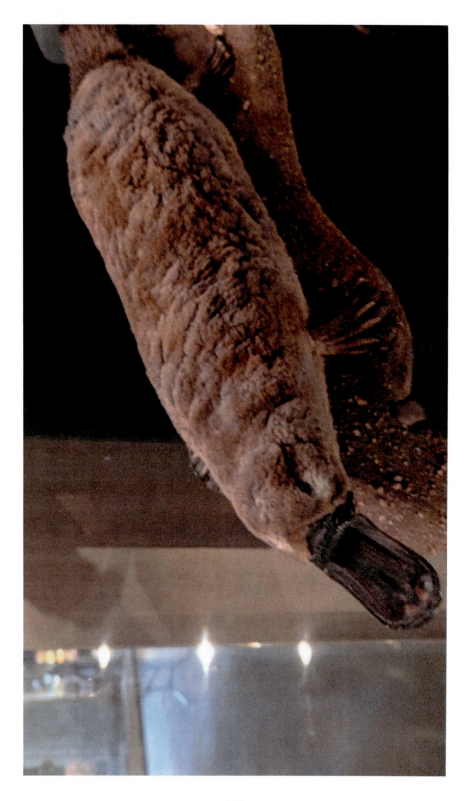

SUITABILITY AS PETS

The Platypus would not be a good choice for a pet. If you want to see them, your local zoo or aquarium might have some that you can watch in a suitable habitat. But creating a habitat for them at your house would be a very difficult thing to do.

COLOR ME

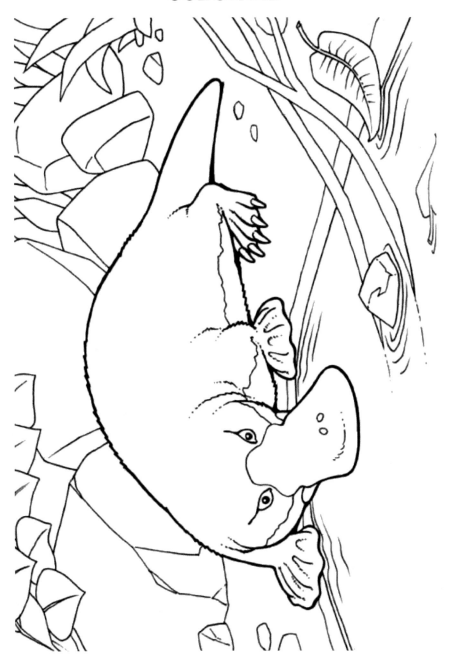

Please leave me a review here:

http://lisastrattin.com/Review-Vol-265

For more Kindle Downloads Visit Lisa Strattin Author Page on Amazon Author Central

http://amazon.com/author/lisastrattin

To see upcoming titles, visit my website at LisaStrattin.com– all books available on kindle!

http://lisastrattin.com

FREE BOOK

FOR ALL SUBSCRIBERS

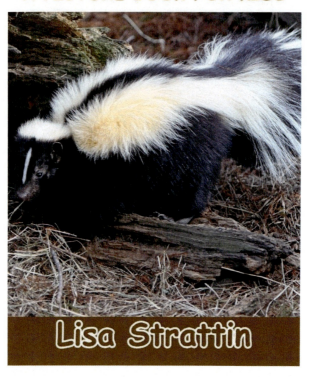

FACTS ABOUT THE
SKUNK

A PICTURE BOOK FOR KIDS

Lisa Strattin

LisaStrattin.com/Subscribe-Here

Made in the USA
Middletown, DE
24 March 2020

87211999R00024